Slumber Wonders

Make All Your Slumber Party Dreams Come True

by Aubre Andrus

illustrated by
Stacy Peterson

Published by American Girl Publishing
Copyright © 2012 by American Girl

Questions or comments? Call 1-800-845-0005,
visit our Web site at **americangirl.com**, or write to Customer Service,
American Girl, 8400 Fairway Place, Middleton, WI 53562-0497.

Printed in China
12 13 14 15 16 17 18 LEO 10 9 8 7 6 5 4 3 2 1

All American Girl marks are trademarks of American Girl.

Editorial Development: Carrie Anton, Trula Magruder, Mary Richards, Jessica Nordskog

Art Direction & Design: Lisa Wilber

Production: Tami Kepler, Sarah Boecher, Jeannette Bailey, Judith Lary

Illustrations: Stacy Peterson

Special thanks to Claire S., Erin E., Devanae A., Chloe K.

Safety Note

All the instructions in this book have been tested. Results from
this testing were incorporated into this book. Nonetheless, all
recommendations and suggestions are made without any
guarantees on the part of American Girl Publishing. Because
of differing tools, ingredients, conditions, and individual skills,
the publisher disclaims liability for any injuries, losses, or other
damages that may result from using the information in this book.

Dear Reader,

The only thing more fun than going to a slumber party is planning one! And when it comes to planning parties, we consider ourselves experts.

In this book, you'll get ideas on everything from what to eat to what to do to what to wear. You'll also find

• all kinds of awesome themes to fit your personality perfectly.

• exciting games and crafts to keep your guests busy for hours.

• delicious recipes for treats that will tickle your guests' taste buds.

We'll tell you how to make your next celebration a super success, from sending out the invitations to bidding your last guest farewell. This book has everything you need to make your slumber party dreams come true. All you need to add are your best buddies and a big smile!

Your friends at American Girl

Contents

Invitation Etiquette

Follow these three simple steps to start the party planning on the right foot.

1. Ask your parents how many guests you can invite. Run the guest list by your parents before making the invitations.

2. Be considerate when passing out invitations to your party. If you can't mail the invitations, give them to your guests privately so no one feels left out.

3. On the invitations, include a start and end time, phone number, and address. Include any special instructions, such as what guests should wear or bring.

Perfect Planning

After you pick the perfect theme, it's time to start making a plan! A week before the party, make a list of all the supplies you need. Start decorating the night before the party so that you don't feel rushed on the big day.

Set the Stage

A snack table allows your guests to grab food whenever they're feeling hungry. Stack plates, bowls, and napkins neatly on the table. Keep water bottles cool and within reach by filling a plastic bin with ice.

Get the Party Started

Before your guests arrive, turn on some music. Make sure the snacks and drinks are ready for guests to enjoy while they wait for others to arrive.

As guests arrive, show them to the room or area where you'll be having the party, and offer to help carry their sleeping bags and pillows.

If some of your guests don't know each other, make introductions right away. When you introduce a friend, say her name, how you know her, and one interesting thing about her. For example, "This is my friend Hannah. She lives next door and has the cutest bulldog named Mervin."

The Happy Hostess

You can plan a general schedule of events for your party, but it's OK to ask guests for their ideas, too. Ask, "Do you want to play another game or eat a snack first?" If guests don't have a preference, then just make a decision yourself.

Make sure everyone feels included! Keep the inside jokes to a minimum if one of your guests isn't in that class.

If something goes wrong at your party, don't worry! The guests will still have fun if you keep a smile on your face.

Parent Patrol

Talk to Mom and Dad before the party so that you know what the ground rules are for your gang, and your parents know what you expect from them. Do you want a parent to hang around to help keep things rolling? Want Mom to step in if an argument crops up? Or would you rather run the show as much as possible? Same goes for siblings. To avoid problems, talk to your whole family in advance about your party.

Super Schedule

Games and crafts will be a lot more fun if you have the time and space to do them. Plan ahead by choosing a few activities that you and your friends will love. Will there be enough time during your party for all of them? Make sure you set aside enough time to do a few activities. Now ask your parents to help choose a place for each game or craft. Is there enough room for everyone to participate comfortably? The more you plan out these details ahead of time, the more smoothly your party will run—and the more fun it will be!

Safety Note

Any time you see this hand or when you think a project or recipe is too hard to do yourself, ask an adult to help you. Be sure an adult supervises any cutting or cooking. Also make sure you keep small pieces, such as beads and rhinestones, put away so younger siblings don't eat them!

The Big Good-Bye

Be sure to thank each of your guests for coming. Before they leave, scour the house for any sleepover supplies or personal items your friends may have left behind. Send each guest home with a party favor.

Cleanup Crew

You should always leave a place cleaner than you found it—that includes the party place! Help your parents take down decorations, do the dishes, and take out the trash. They're more likely to let you have another sleepover if you lend a helping hand.

Glam-a-Pajama

**It's a silly slumber party
full of sparkle and smiles!**

Invitation

Cut cute mismatched pajama shapes from patterned scrapbook paper. Glue a plain T-shirt shape to a patterned pant cutout and write the party information on the T-shirt. Ask guests to bring an old pillowcase to use for a craft.

You're invited to a Pajama Party!

Friday 7p.m. at Hannah's house

Pillowcase Pouch

Use an old pillowcase for this craft. Draw a shape, such as a star, on a piece of fleece. Place the shape on top of another color of fleece and trace around it, leaving a border. Cut it out. Repeat until you have a stack of 4 different sizes with smallest on top and biggest on bottom. Using fabric glue, attach the shapes to the pillowcase. Let dry. Tie a ribbon around the bag to close it. Use the bag for your next slumber party.

Sleepy-Time Headband

Keep your hair from getting too messy while you sleep. Tightly tie ribbons into tiny bows around a stretchy head-band. Trim the ends of the ribbons.

Sleeping-Bag Zipper Pull

Cut felt into shapes and use fabric glue to attach the layers together. Cut a slit near the top and string a ribbon through. Tie it to your zipper and trim the ends.

Colorful Cake

Turn a plain cake into a colorful masterpiece! Press small chewy candies onto a store-bought vanilla-frosted cake. Keep the cake in the refrigerator until guests arrive.

Citrus Cooler

In a blender, combine 3 cups vanilla frozen yogurt with 3 cups orange juice. Ask an adult to blend well. Pour into glasses. Serves 2 to 3.

Pajama Jam

Hold a pajama fashion show!
Walk down a pretend catwalk
to music. Don't forget to smile
for the camera!

15

Bright Barrettes

Cut a strip of nonadhesive VELCRO® brand hook-and-loop fasteners into small squares. Glue rhinestones to one of the flat sides. Let dry. To use, separate squares, place a thin layer of hair in between the squares, and press together.

Fuzzy Feet

Turn a pair of flip-flops into silly slippers. Trace each flip-flop onto fleece. Cut out the shapes, and cut a slit where the thong needs to fit. Glue the fleece to the flip-flop. Glue a craft boa to the thong. Let dry.

Groovy Moves

Girls stand in a line with their eyes covered. No one opens her eyes until she has been tapped on the shoulder. The girl at one end starts by opening her eyes, tapping the girl next to her, showing her a dance move, and then covering her eyes. The second girl taps the third girl, shows her the first dance move, adds her own dance move, and covers her eyes again. Keep passing the dance on until everyone has added a move. The last girl says, "Eyes open!" and shows everyone the entire dance routine.

Glitzy Goodies

Make a brush beautiful by gluing rhinestones to the back of a mini hairbrush. Let dry. Do the same to a mini mirror.

Hilarious Hairdos

Ask guests to sit in a circle. Each girl turns to the person on her right. In the middle of the circle is a pile of new, unused hair accessories—headbands, barrettes, and hair elastics. On "Go!" everyone must style the hair of the girl in front of her in only 5 minutes. You can't check the hairstyle from the front to see how it looks—just try to make the silliest hairstyle you can! Be careful not to pull or tangle anyone's hair.

Bedtime Story

This game is fun to play when you're snug in your sleeping bags. Start the game by passing a stuffed animal to a nearby girl. Every time you get the stuffed animal, you have to add one word to the story. See how long—and silly—your bedtime story gets. No sleeping until the story is over!

Girl Gab

Get to know your guests better by having each girl answer the following questions:

1. If you could be a guest star on an episode of a TV show, which show would you choose?
2. What would you do FOR a million dollars?
3. What would you do WITH a million dollars?
4. If you could have dinner with someone famous, who would it be?
5. Stop. Think. What's under your bed? 'Fess up!
6. Name your top pick for movie night.
7. What was your favorite thing about kindergarten?
8. What name would you like instead of your own?
9. What is your biggest fear?
10. Who would you most like to trade places with?

Fancy Farewells

Help your guests keep the party going by giving them a small gift bag filled with lots of glam. Include a small hairbrush, a hand mirror, and sparkly hair accessories.

Megan

Critter Shindig

This party is the perfect way to feature creatures, from favorite pets to amazing animals!

Invitation

Cut a square shape from a piece of textured cardstock. This will be the back of the invitation, where you fill in all the party details. For this party, ask guests to bring a stuffed animal for a game. Next, trace the square paper onto leopard- or tiger-print felt (available at craft stores). Cut out the felt shape and glue the wrong side of the felt to the back of the card. On the felt, write "You're Invited!" using dimensional fabric paint. Let dry.

Decorations

Mix and match animal-print tablecloths, plates, and cups. Create big pawprints out of paper by cutting 1 big circle and 3 smaller ones. Ask a parent if it's OK to tape them to the walls and floor. Create "tracks" for your guests to follow from the front door to the party room.

Furry Friend Fashion Show

Challenge your guests to create fantastic fashions for their stuffed animals with only felt, scissors, ribbon, and rhinestones. Set a time limit, then hold a stuffed animal fashion show! Guests can walk down the runway and show off their stylish creations.

Pet ID Tags

Make a collar for your stuffed animal. Decorate metal-rimmed paper tags (found at office supply or hardware stores) with markers and stickers and hang from a bright ribbon. Write your stuffed animal's name on the tag.

23

Fish Food

Ask an adult to make blue gelatin by following the directions on the box. Once the gelatin has cooled, pour evenly into clear plastic cups, and place cups on a tray in the refrigerator until firm. Before serving, press a few gummy fish into the gelatin.

Animal Chow

Create a snack mix medley of animal-shaped cookies and crackers. Look for rabbits, goldfish, and zoo animals in the snack aisle of your grocery store.

Cupcake Critters

Make cupcakes look like your favorite furry friends with frosting, candy, and sprinkles. For a base, add a small drop of food coloring to frosting or a plastic bag of coconut to create the shade you need. After frosting the cupcake, decorate with candy or sprinkle with colored shredded coconut. For creature features, make ears out of marshmallows or gummy candy. Small hard candies and gel make perfect eyes. Sprinkles are great for whiskers. Make a nose or beak from chewy candy. Make the candy easier to bend and tear by warming it in your hands first.

Heads . . .

Turn a pack of plastic headbands into
animal disguises. Fold a piece of felt in
half and cut ears along the fold. (When
folded, there should be a front layer
and a back layer to the ear.) Loop
the ear around the top of a
headband and glue the two
layers together. Repeat for
the second ear.

. . . or Tails

Add ferocious flair to a ponytail. Tie
lengths of animal-print ribbon or
long strips of printed felt in knots
around an elastic band.

Animal Noise Bingo

For this game, each player will need 9 stickers featuring 9 to 12 different animal images throughout the group. Each animal used must be one with an obvious noise associated with it. You'll also need 18 to 24 table tennis balls (available where sporting goods are sold). Place one animal sticker on each ball and use 2 table tennis balls per animal. Then place the balls in a bowl.

On a sheet of construction paper, draw a grid that has 3 rows and 3 columns. Make a grid for each guest. Players place animal stickers on their sheets (one sticker per square). Players can use animals more than once, but no more than twice per card. Hand out 9 pennies or buttons to each player to use as playing pieces.

To play, guests take turns drawing a table tennis ball from the bowl. Instead of announcing the name of the animal, the girl must make the animal noise. Anyone who has that animal on her sheet makes the noise back and places a playing piece on that space on her grid.

Whoever gets 3 animals in a row announces her win by standing up and making the 3 animal noises in a row.

27

Creature Koozies

Each guest will need felt, dimensional fabric paint, glue, and scissors. Cut a strip of animal-print felt that is long enough to wrap around a cup or water bottle. With either cut-out shapes of felt or dimensional paint, make a face in the middle of the strip of felt. Let dry. Attach VELCRO® brand adhesive hook-and-loop fasteners to the front of one end of the strip and the back of the other end of the strip. It's a wrap!

Doggie Bags

Like those once used for leftovers from a restaurant, doggie bags make the perfect sack for guests to bring home the animal fun. On small white paper bags, stamp pawprints. Then fill the bags with cute critter stuff such as inexpensive animal face masks, animal stickers, animal-shaped candy, and animal pencil toppers.

Camping Bash

Bring the outdoors in while still sleeping
under the stars and eating s'more snacks.

Invitation

Pitch a paper tent to hand deliver to all your happy camper guests. Start with a 7-by-7-inch square of double-sided scrapbook paper, making sure one side is lightly colored enough to write on. Leaving a 1-inch border around the sides, fill in your party details. Be sure to tell campers to bring their sleeping bags and pillows.

To fold the tent:

1. Lay the paper so that the party wording is facing you. Fold the square in half. Unfold.

2. Fold one set of corners together, making half an X from the 2 folds. Unfold the paper and repeat with the remaining corners.

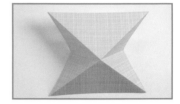

3. Fold the paper in half, tucking the sides of the paper into the center so that it forms a triangle.

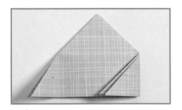

4. Fold the bottom corners of the triangle toward the center so that the points meet in the middle along the bottom edge. This is the back, and the folded corners can act as a stand.

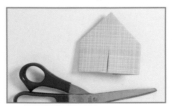

5. On the tent's front side, cut about a 1.5-inch slit from the bottom straight edge toward the middle peak.

6. Fold back the corners made by the cut to look like the opening of the tent. Deliver the tent invitation as is, or decorate the tent with other paper and sticker embellishments.

Twinkle, Twinkle

At a party store, buy navy blue balloons filled with helium. Cut yellow stars from construction paper, and punch a hole in each star. Use clear string in different lengths to tie a couple stars to the ends of each balloon. Let the balloons float around the party room to create a shooting star setting. *(Tip: Helium lasts about 24 hours, so buy or fill the balloons the day of your party.)*

Cool Campfire

Decorate the food table with a mini campfire that is sure not to burn! Layer a few sheets of orange, yellow, and red tissue paper. Squeeze the center of the sheets at the bottom, and cut the tops into flame shapes. Make logs from cinnamon sticks, and set the tissue paper flames on top.

Bug Juice

No camping trip is complete without this classic drink. Mix a packet of unsweetened lemon-lime drink mix with 3 cups of ginger ale and 3 cups of lemon-lime soda. Finish with a few handfuls of ice cubes and a few big scoops of lime sherbet. Stir the bug juice before serving to make it fizz.

Dinky Dogs

Ask an adult to microwave mini hot dogs (look for appetizer-sized beef smoked sausage at the grocery store) for 30–45 seconds. Stick a food-safe mini craft stick into the sausage for a just-roasted-on-the-campfire look.

Indoor S'mores

Top plain chocolate cupcakes with marshmallow fluff. Place graham cracker cereal in a plastic bag and tap lightly with a spoon to break the cereal into bits. Sprinkle the crushed graham cracker mix on top, and finish with mini chocolate chips.

Dirt Parfait

In small clear cups, alternate scoops of chocolate pudding with crushed chocolate sandwich cookies. (Crush the cookies by placing a handful in a plastic bag and tapping lightly with a spoon until they crumble.) Finish with gummy worms on top!

Soft Sit-Upon

Have campers create some cozy seats. Place a 14-by-14-inch foam pad (available at craft stores) between 2 bandannas. Tie the corners of the 2 bandannas together. Use the sit-upon on the floor or in a tent.

Campfire Chatter

Sit in a circle and set a battery-operated lantern in the middle of it. Divide up a stack of blank note cards and ask everyone to write something completely random on each one—the name of a person, a favorite place, or a thing. Now take turns telling stories. When it's your turn, draw a card and incorporate that card into your story. See how silly your story can get!

Crafty Camp Tees

Give each guest a plain, colored T-shirt. As a group, come up with a camp name and logo. Using fabric markers, draw the logo for your camp on each shirt. Then take turns signing the other campers' shirts. You can even write a number or name for your "bunk" and hang a sign outside your sleeping area. *(Note: Put a piece of cardboard inside the shirt to keep the markers from bleeding though.)*

Decorated Flashlights

Create personalized camping accessories to light up the night and glimmer in the day. Have your campers decorate inexpensive flashlights using adhesive rhinestones, glow-in-the-dark stickers, and glow-in-the-dark dimensional craft paint. Let dry.

Sleeping Bag Shuffle

In this sleeping bag shuffle, it's every camper for herself. Lay all the sleeping bags on the floor. The goal of the game is to roll up and tie as many sleeping bags as possible in one minute. Ask one person to be the timekeeper. Let each girl play the game one at a time.

Bright Night Favors

Fill empty water bottles with sheets of glow-in-the-dark stickers and plastic stars for guests to take when they leave.

Sweet Soiree

**Dazzling desserts and sugary snacks
are the stars of this sweet feast.**

Invitation

Turn a batch of store-bought or home-made sugar cookies into invitations that you can hand deliver to your friends. Use gel to write "You're Invited!" on a cookie with gel. Let gel harden overnight. Slip the "You're Invited!" cookie plus a few additional cookies into a plastic treat bag. Tie the top with a ribbon, and attach a tag with the party details.

Saturday 7 p.m. @ Pippa's

You're Invited!

Party Pose

Fill a bowl with candy bracelets, necklaces, and rings. Let guests play dress-up, and then snap a sweet photo of the whole party.

Sweet Sprinkles and Candy Curtain

Confetti sprinkled on top of a plain white, brown, or pink tablecloth will turn any tabletop into a cupcake-like delight.

Make a candy curtain by tying wrapped candies and candies with holes in the center to long lengths of curling ribbon. Hang over a door, and tie a few candies as a weight on the opposite side.

Fruity Fun

Set out colorful berries and yogurt in brightly colored dishes with sugar cones nearby. Guests can fill the cones by spooning in their favorite mixture of fruits and yogurt.

39

Candy Box Purses

Each guest will need a movie-theater-sized box of candy, ribbon, Glue Dots®, and a small VELCRO® brand adhesive hook-and-loop closure.

1. Carefully open side ends of the box, but not the top and bottom. Empty the contents.

2. Cut a V-shaped flap from the top left corner to the top right corner.

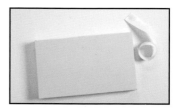

3. Reassemble the sides of the box with Glue Dots.

4. Cut a length of ribbon for the handle and attach to the inside of the box with Glue Dots.

5. Cut a small length of ribbon and attach it to the inside of the flap with a Glue Dot.

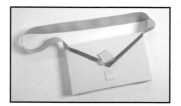

6. Attach one side of a small VELCRO® brand adhesive hook-and-loop closure to the end of the ribbon and the other side to the bottom of the box.

Pretty Punch

Mix a few batches of colorful drink mix in bright colors like blue, green, and pink. Pour some of the liquid into ice-cube trays. Let freeze overnight. At the party, let guests create pretty punch and ice cube combinations. Finish with a colored straw.

Sundae Surprise

Since this party is for dessert lovers only, why not combine two of the best treats—whipped cream and cupcakes? Drizzle chocolate sauce onto store-bought or homemade vanilla cupcakes. Finish with a squirt of whipped cream, sprinkles, and a cherry on top.

41

Sweet Sprints

Break into 2 teams and set up a series of really yummy relays. Here are 3 games to try:

- Players on each team take turns using chopsticks to move one gummy candy from one bowl into another bowl 10 steps away.

- Each player holds a plastic spoon. Players on each team spread apart equal distance from one another. To win, a team must pass a gumball from one end of the line to the other—using only the spoons—before the other team does.

- Each team starts with a big bag of multicolored candy. On "Go!" each team must separate the candy by color as fast as they can.

Creative Cookie Challenge

Divide into teams of 2. Line up tubs of frosting, icing, and bowls of sprinkles and candy. On "Go!" one girl from each team has 3 minutes to decorate a sugar cookie—the catch is that she must keep her eyes closed! Her team member can give her directions. At the end of 3 minutes, switch roles. Give each guest an award at the end of the competition. For example: Tastiest Treat, Quickest Creation, and Coolest Cookie.

Sprinkle Storm

Colorful balloons act as giant sprinkles in this game. Give each guest one balloon. On "Go!" players throw the balloons in the air and try to keep them off the ground. If all balloons stay in the air for 1 minute, everyone moves on to round 2. This time add 1 more balloon to the mix. See how many rounds you can play!

Nickname Game

Write sweet but silly nicknames on adhesive tags (white mailing labels decorated with cute cupcake stickers work nicely). Place the tags in a bowl and let each guest pick an alias when she arrives. Here are some ideas:

- Muffin
- Candy
- Sugar
- Sweetheart
- Buttercup
- Cookie
- Gumdrop
- Honey
- Pudding

Bon-Bon Voyage

Give each guest a colorful metal tin (found at craft stores). Let guests fill their tins with any leftover sweet treats.

Drive-in Diner Party

Throw a fabulous bash with a 1950s twist
and delicious diner details.

Invitation

Buy small records at a secondhand store, or cut out circles from a sheet of black foam to look like records. Cut 2 circles from colored scrapbook paper so that they cover the center of the record (front and back). Write the details of your party on the scrapbook paper. Then glue the paper circles to the middle of the record. Hand deliver the records to your guests.

Diner Decorations

Cover a table with a black-and-white checkered tablecloth. Sprinkle music note confetti on top. Make a place setting for each person with red and black plates, cups, napkins, and utensils. Decorate the cups with music note stickers.

Ponytail Station

When each guest arrives, give her a 1950s makeover!
Set up a chair for a quick stop at the beauty shop.
If she has long hair, put it up in a ponytail and tie
a ribbon or sheer strip of fabric into a knot around
her ponytail. If she has short hair, tie a strip of fabric
around her head like a headband with a knot at the
nape of her neck.

47

Letter Sweaters

To complete the 1950s look, let each guest make a felt letter (the letter of her first name) to attach to her shirt. Cut out a letter from felt, then glue it to another piece of felt in a different color. Cut around the edges, leaving a little bit of a colored border. Use craft-strength Glue Dots® to attach the letter to each girl's top.

Shake Stand

Serve mini milk shakes in small glasses so your guests can sample different flavors. Below are some recipes to try. Make sure to top each one with whipped cream and a cherry.

- ★Banana Blast: Ask an adult to mix 1 banana, 2 scoops of vanilla ice cream, and ½ cup milk in a blender.
- Root Beer Float: Add a scoop of vanilla ice cream to each glass, and top with root beer.
- ★Chocolate Cherry Dream: Ask an adult to mix 2 big scoops of chocolate ice cream and ½ cup cherry soda in a blender.

Jukebox Jams

Check out a few 1950s rock-and-roll CDs from the library and ask an adult or sibling to DJ the party.

Diner Dinner

Nothing says "diner" like burgers and fries! Ask a parent to cook up some bite-sized sliders and fries.

Speed Tables

Players break into 2 teams. Each team must set a table as quickly as possible. Assign each team member one item: utensils, plates, cups, napkins, etc. Ask an adult to time each team. On "Go!" each player must perform her task and tag the next player when she's done. Whichever team gets the fastest time wins!

Diner Dash

Break into 2 teams. Each team needs a tray and the same number of props—try fake food, empty plastic cups, plastic utensils, and paper plates. Players must take turns carrying the tray with 1 hand, from one side of the room to the other and back again, without dropping anything. Players then pass the tray to the next girl in line. If a player drops anything, she must start over.

Savvy Server

Take turns pretending to be the server and pretending to be the hungry diners. One player is the server, and the other players sit around a table. The server must take everyone's order (without writing it down), one at a time. The guests can order any kind of food they'd like. When the group is done placing their orders, the server must repeat everyone's order out loud. See who has the best memory!

Eggroll
Wonton Soup
Sweet and Sour Chicken

Corn Dog
Macaroni and Cheese
Chocolate Brownie

Chips and Salsa
Burrito
Enchilada

Caesar Salad
Cheese Ravioli
Tiramisu

Blueberry Pancakes
Bacon
Hash Browns

Sock Hop Socks

Have guests make no-slip socks so they can dance at the next sock hop worry free. Give each girl a pair of plain socks. On a covered surface, have guests use fabric paint to decorate the soles so they become nonslip. Let dry overnight.

Thanks with a Twist

Using a 2-inch circle paper punch, create enough circles from scrapbook paper as there are guests. Ask a parent to help you cut 2 small parallel slits in the top and bottom of the circle. Write "Thanks!" in the center of the circle. Slip the circle onto the straight end of a curlique straw through the slits. Place all the straws in a cup, and have guests each grab one when they leave.

Personalized Party

Everything at this party features names, initials, or faces of you and your guests!

LOLA

SOPHIE

HANNAH

CHRISTEL

Invitation

Make a name bracelet for each guest by stringing letter beads (available at craft stores) onto a cord. Write the details of your party on a paper tag, and ask your guests to bring as many small school photos as there are guests invited (or color copies of their photos). String the bracelet through a hole in the tag, and tie a loose knot.

Guest Garland

String up a letter garland created with your guests' initials. Cut triangles from felt and attach them to a ribbon with Glue Dots. Attach felt letter stickers (found at craft stores) to the triangles. Ask a parent to help you hang the garland in the party room.

Custom Cookies

Before your guests arrive, frost store-bought or homemade sugar cookies with vanilla frosting, and top with sprinkles. Then spell out your guests' names on the cookies with gel frosting or alphabet-shaped cereal. Use the cookies as place settings so that guests know where to sit.

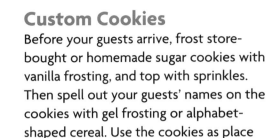

Me Magnets

Turn a few sets of store-bought plastic alphabet magnets into lovely letters. Let guests choose their name, a word they like, or just a single letter and decorate with adhesive rhinestones, dimensional craft paint, and stickers. Let dry.

55

Alphabet Soup

Before the party, take a trip to the grocery store in search of any food in the shape of the alphabet to serve. Keep your eyes peeled for cereal, pasta noodles, or soups loaded with letters!

Cake Face

Give each guest a plain frosted cupcake. Challenge each girl to turn the cupcake into a self-portrait with decorating gel, sprinkles, slim licorice rope (the kind you peel), and candy. Vote on which cupcake looks most like the girl.

Special Signs

Give each guest a wood or cardboard letter (found at craft stores) that is the first letter of her first name. Provide scraps of patterned paper and Mod Podge® for guests to decorate their letters. Let dry on a paper plate. Loop a ribbon through the letter or attach a loop to the back with Glue Dots so that guests can hang their letters at home.

Personalized Pouch

Dress up plain tote bags (found at craft stores) with a big letter. Have each guest trace her first initial onto a piece of patterned fabric. Cut out the letter, and then use fabric glue to attach it to the bag. Let dry. Have all the guests autograph each other's bags using fabric markers.

Friend Frame

Turn foam sheets and clothespins into a personalized friend frame. Each guest will need school photos of a few of the other guests, foam sheets, glue, and mini spring clothespins.

1. Cut a rectangular strip from a foam sheet that's big enough to fit all the school photos you want to include.

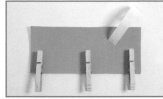

2. Attach the closed side of 2 or 3 mini clothespins to the back of the foam with Glue Dots to act as legs.

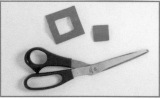

3. Cut school-photo-sized circles and squares from foam.

4. Fold the frame in half, and cut out the center.

5. Glue the frame on top of a school photo, and trim the edges.

6. Glue the back of the photo to the front of the foam rectangle.

Letter Stories

Each guest must tell a made-up story about herself for an entire minute using as many words as she can that start with the first letter of her first name. For example:

> Madison loves to wear moccasins and make movies. She lives in a mansion, and most of her months are spent making music on her mandolin.

Word Warp

Guests break into teams of 2 and then pick out the letters in their names from a bag of letter beads. Decide if you'll play first names only or first and last names. On "Go!" teams have 1 minute to make as many words as they can from their beads. At the end of the minute, the winner is the team who created the most words. If there's a tie, see who created the longest word.

Guessing Game

Give each guest 5 note cards. On each card, have guests use their nondominant hand to write one thing about themselves that others might not know. Have guests sit in a circle; then shuffle the cards and place them facedown in the center of the circle. Each player draws a card, reads it to herself, guesses who wrote it, and sets it facedown in front of the person she guessed. Play continues until all the cards have been placed. Then each girl reads the cards in her pile aloud, saying whether or not each one is hers. If it isn't, she puts it back in the center pile. The guessing continues until all the cards from the center pile are gone.

Good-Bye Goodies

Decorate paper bags with the names of your guests. Fill the bags with letter stickers, a fabric marker, a stamp, and letter beads so that your friends can personalize their own things at home.

Petite Party

**A celebration that's miniature-sized
in everything but the fun!**

Invitation

Create your own mini mail delivery with this petite package! Buy small cardboard jewelry boxes from a craft store. Cut a piece of colored paper into a small rectangle and then fold it in half to make a card. Decorate the card with markers and a small adhesive rhinestone. Write the details of the party inside. Slip the card into the box and finish with a tiny sheet of tissue paper. Decorate the lid with your guest's address and a sticker for a stamp. Tie a thin ribbon around the box and make a bow. Hand deliver the invitations.

Decorations

Small party balloons and paper streamers cut in half will make your party more petite. Serve food on snack plates and drinks in 3-ounce paper or plastic cups.

Pixie Punch

Place a small scoop of raspberry sherbet in the bottom of a 3-ounce cup. Top with sparkling white grape juice and finish with a bendable straw cut in half.

Cutest Cupcakes

Before your guests arrive, ask an adult to help you bake a batch of chocolate and vanilla mini cupcakes, or buy some from a store. Decorate cupcakes with different combinations of frosting, sprinkles, and gel.

Bunny Slippers

No petite PJ party is complete without a sweet pair of small bunny slippers.

1. ✋⭐ On **wax paper,** flatten a large **marshmallow** with your hands, and cut it in half with **food scissors.**

2. Dip cut sides of marshmallows in **colored sugar** to prevent stickiness.

3. Press your finger into the marshmallow to make the inside of a slipper. (Dip finger in sugar if it's sticky.)

4. Spread **frosting** across the toe and around the sides of the slipper. Then dip it in **white nonpareils** to cover the frosting.

5. Attach nonpareil eyes and nose with frosting. For ears, cut a **mini marshmallow** in half. Press the cut side in sugar, and attach the ears with frosting.

Bite-Sized Buffet

⭐ Create a collection of tiny treats.

- Find bite-sized versions of your favorite crackers and cookies at the grocery store.

- Turn English muffins into personal pizzas with pasta sauce and shredded cheese sprinkled on top. Ask a parent to micro-wave for 45 seconds. Let cool.

- Ask an adult to make miniature pancakes for breakfast. Serve with store-bought mini doughnuts and small cups of orange juice.

Pocket Books

Stack 5 pieces of plain white paper and one piece of patterned paper. Cut the layers into a rectangle shape and then fold the stack in half. Lay ribbon along the fold. Take the ends of the ribbon and tie in a tight bow at the outside of the book. Use your books like a guest book and sign each other's with short and sweet messages.

Tiny Fruit Earrings

Roll a small piece of nontoxic air-modeling clay (found at craft stores) in your hands to warm it up and make it easier to shape. Form it into mini fruit shapes. Let dry overnight. In the morning, use tacky glue to attach your mini fruit to hypoallergenic earring-stud blanks (found at craft stores in the jewelry aisle). Let dry.

Mini Makeover

Take turns braiding a mini braid into each other's hair. Secure with a small elastic band, and finish with a thin ribbon tied into a tiny bow.

Baby Buckets Game

Attach three 3-ounce paper cups to a craft stick evenly spaced in a straight line. Set on a tabletop and ask guests to take a few steps back. Using a table tennis ball, players must first land the ball in the first cup. If they make it, they move on to the second cup and so on. If they make it to the third cup, give them a little prize.

Bitty Basketball Shoot-Out

To make a mini basketball hoop, cut off the bottom half of a 3-ounce paper cup. Use a Glue Dot to attach a craft stick to the back of the cup. Cut a rectangle from foam for the backboard and attach it to the top of the craft stick with a Glue Dot.

To play, you'll need one player to hold the basket and one player to shoot a table tennis ball from a few steps away. There are lots of different variations on Bitty Basketball: *(Note: Some games need more than one basketball hoop.)*

• See how many baskets each girl can shoot in 1 minute.

• Break into 2 teams and have a relay race. Each player must make a basket before the next player can shoot.

• Break into teams of 2. First team to get 5 baskets is the Bitty Basketball champion.

Tiny Takeaways

Fill a small paper gift bag with mini accessories, including stickers, lip gloss, barrettes, and travel-sized lotion.

Pretend Hotel Sleepover

**Invite your friends to a special stay
at a "faux"-tel—designed exclusively by you!**

Invitation

Design your invitation to look like a hotel brochure. Name the hotel after yourself, such as "Hotel Claire." Write "You're invited to spend a fabulous night at Hotel Claire" and include all the party details inside.

The Lobby

Pick a room to be the lobby. Play classical music softly in the background. When your guests arrive, point them in the direction of the check-in counter—a table or desk that you set up before the party. Ask a parent to sign in your guests. Ask a sibling to be the bellhop and lead your guests to their suite while carrying their luggage.

Room Decor

Make pretend hotel room numbers and signs. You can also make a sign with fake buttons for the "elevator" (stairs). Give your bedroom a name, such as "Super Special Suite," and hang a pretty decorated sign.

The Five-Star Restaurant

Ask a parent or sibling to be the chef—he or she can even dress up—and ring a bell when it's time for dinner. Lead your guests to their seats in the "restaurant," where the "chef" will serve dinner and dessert. While everyone is eating, ask a parent or sibling to place wrapped chocolates on all of the guests' pillows.

Packing Challenge

See how good your guests are at packing —with their eyes closed! Pick 2 players, and give each one a suitcase and an equal pile of folded clothes, such as 5 pairs of jeans, 5 shirts, and 3 pairs of shoes. Keeping her eyes closed, each player packs as quickly and neatly as she can for 1 minute. The fullest and neatest suitcase wins!

Fresh Faces

Nothing says spa more than a face mask! Whip up a batch of oatmeal-yogurt mask before your guests arrive and leave it covered in the fridge until you need it.

To make: Mix 2 tablespoons of plain yogurt with 2 tablespoons of uncooked oatmeal. *(Note: This recipe makes enough for one face mask. You'll need to increase the recipe so that you have enough for all your guests.)*

After all guests apply the mask, be sure to get a photo! Let the mask dry for 10 minutes (or sooner if anyone's face starts to itch or feels really tight). For real relaxation while the mask is drying, have each guest place cucumber slices over each eyelid. Ahhh!

Spa Spray

A few hours before the party, ask an adult to cut up a cucumber and place the slices in a pitcher of water. Let sit in the refrigerator until needed. At the party, let each guest fill a plastic 3-ounce travel spray bottle with the mixture. Lightly spray it on your face for a refreshing finish for a scented slumber. Empty the bottles at the end of the party.

Take-a-Break Relaxation Masks

Each girl will need a piece of felt, dimensional fabric paint, ribbon, and rhinestones. Cut an eye mask shape from felt. Fold the left and right side slightly and snip a small slit for the ribbon. Decorate the mask with dimensional fabric paint and adhesive rhinestones. Let dry. String a long piece of ribbon through the front of one slit, behind the eye mask, and back up through the slit on the other side until the two ends of the ribbon are even. Place on your head and ask a friend to tie the ribbon in a bow at the nape of your neck. Wear for some quick quiet time during a pedicure or manicure.

Sleeping Sign

Using the tear-out door hanger in the back of the book, color in each side and write in the name of your hotel. Hang it on the outside of the door of the room where you and your guests will be sleeping.

Suite Treats

In your "suite," display snack-sized versions of your favorite treats on a tray. Try mini water bottles, individually packaged cookies and crackers, and bite-sized candy bars.

water

nuts

chocolate

Midnight Movie

Let your guests "rent" a movie from the hotel. Display your 5 favorite movies and let guests vote on the movie they want to watch. Present the movie with a big bowl of freshly popped popcorn, cups of soda, and movie-theater-sized boxes of candy.

Breakfast Buffet

Let guests plate their own pancakes and choose from a variety of toppings, such as chocolate chips, raspberries, and sliced strawberries, plus syrup and powdered sugar. Set up a beverage bar with milk, apple juice, and orange juice.

SYRUP

Parting Packages

Wrap travel-sized soap, shampoo, and conditioner in a square of tulle and tie closed with a ribbon bow. Leave one of these packages in the "suite" for each guest.

Conditioner

Shampoo

Soap

More Dream Themes

PINK

Pretty in Pink
Paint your party pink! Ask guests to wear their favorite shade of pink from head to toe and give prizes for outfits, such as Most Creative and Most Pink. Serve pink lemonade, pink cotton candy, and, of course, a pretty pink cake!

Winter Carnival
It may be cold outside, but that won't freeze out the fun for this party! Organize an afternoon of sledding or ice-skating. For favors, use dimensional fabric paint to personalize a set of stretchy knit gloves for each guest. End the party with a steaming cup of hot chocolate and marshmallows!

Paris Party
Invite your guests to a pretend trip to France! Serve croissants and crêpes and play French music (check out a CD at the library). Give guests French-braid makeovers and favor bags with mini French flags and stickers.

Flower Fiesta

The perfect spring party is in bloom! Decorate with flower power—fake flower garlands, tissue paper flower centerpieces, and flower stickers on cups. Turn sugar cookies into pretty flowers with marshmallow petals and gumdrop centers.

Pep Rally

Invite your team over to show some spirit. Set the stage with streamers and balloons in your team colors. Make spirited hair bands by tying strips of ribbon in your team colors to an elastic band. Create a cheer that will energize the team before the next big game or competition.

Out-of-This-World Party

It's a party planet! Give each guest an alien-like headband decorated with googly eyes. For decorations, turn balloons into planets using markers, and cut paper into shooting stars. Serve freeze-dried treats just like real astronauts eat!